THE FRIENDSHIP CHALLENGE

THE
FRIENDSHIP
CHALLENGE

A Six-Week Guide to True Reconciliation—

One Friendship at a Time

TIM SCOTT & TREY GOWDY

TYNDALE
MOMENTUM®

The nonfiction imprint of
Tyndale House Publishers, Inc.

Visit Tyndale online at www.tyndale.com.

Visit Tyndale Momentum online at www.tyndalemomentum.com.

TYNDALE, Tyndale Momentum, and Tyndale's quill logo are registered trademarks of Tyndale House Publishers, Inc. The Tyndale Momentum logo is a trademark of Tyndale House Publishers, Inc. Tyndale Momentum is the nonfiction imprint of Tyndale House Publishers, Inc., Carol Stream, Illinois.

For information about special discounts for bulk purchases, please contact Tyndale House Publishers at csresponse@tyndale.com, or call 1-800-323-9400.

ISBN 978-1-4964-3068-7

Printed in the United States of America

24   23   22   21   20   19   18
7   6   5   4   3   2   1

Contents

Introduction

OVER THE PAST SEVERAL YEARS, the very foundation of our melting-pot society in America has been shaken—ironically, by our differences. For generations, people have come to "the land of opportunity" to forge a new way of life. They have embraced the American ideals of life, liberty, and the pursuit of happiness and have blended their distinct cultural strengths and values into the larger free society. It has never been perfect, and there have certainly been some rocky points along the way, but generally it has worked out for the common good, and our nation has been strengthened by our united pursuit of harmony within diversity. But lately it seems as if an increasing number of people are choosing to distinguish themselves based on *identity* or *ideology*. We've always been a nation of different people living alongside one another, but now it seems as if we've become more interested in dividing over our differences than in learning how to get along.

TREY

One thing I have learned from my time in Washington, DC, is that conflict is a business model. It *sells*. But it doesn't solve anything. If we want to move from our current conflict-driven environment to one that is based more on *contrast*—that is, an appropriate and necessary recognition of our differences, but without the anger, frustration, and intentional divisiveness that come with conflict—we must first recognize that most people have most things in common. It doesn't make sense that we tend to run toward the things that divide us, while skipping over all the things we agree on.

People often look to government to solve problems in our society. But even though we can pass laws to compel people to change their conduct, no piece of legislation can change someone's heart. There's no law that can make people care about each other. That has to come from someplace other than government. To me, that someplace else is friendship.

I believe that friendship has the best chance of transforming our world. If we will just take the time to hear other people out, seek first to understand, and work together toward mutually agreeable solutions, we have a chance to make a positive difference in each other's lives and in the world around us. We may still disagree strongly about some issues, but if we will commit ourselves to being friends at the beginning of the conversation and friends at the end of the conversation, no matter what, we can work through our differences.

The great things we all want for our future won't happen in Washington, DC. But they can happen in small groups and in local settings where relationships are built. That's the genius of who we are as human beings. That's the genius of how our Creator wired us. We are hardwired for relationships, and as we connect with each other, we find the miracle of problem-solving and reconciliation in the midst of those connections.

In Matthew 18:20, Jesus says, "Where two or three are gathered together in my name, there am I in the midst of them."[1] That's a powerful formula.

TIM

I am very hopeful about our future as a nation, but real and lasting change can begin only through committed friendships that reach across lines of division. I agree with Trey that politics is not how we're going to change the world. We can change the world only by changing people's hearts—through the transforming power of love. The Bible is very clear that love is not just an emotion; it is a *commandment* and a *commitment*. Friendship is born out of the principles of unconditional love and acceptance. Love and acceptance are not situational. They are consistent.

We open the door to reconciliation when we become willing to step outside our comfort zones and try some things that may seem awkward at first—such as initiating a conversation with someone who is different from us. Most of the exciting adventures I've had didn't start off being fun—they were hard. But what's hard becomes easier, so let's be willing to do the hard things so we can enjoy the benefits, rather than doing only the easy things and paying the price.

In the coming days, I hope our nation will continue to be a beacon of hope and opportunity for the world to see. And I hope the church will be at the forefront, finding ways to come together and reveal the true meaning of the body of Christ. Different parts, different likes, different passions, different perspectives, without question; but all woven together by the thread of love and unconditional acceptance of one another. Love and acceptance are also what enable us to share the gospel in fresh, new ways—with words, without words—everywhere we go, and with everyone we meet.

With our book, *Unified: How Our Unlikely Friendship Gives Us Hope for a Divided Country*, and with this discussion guide, Trey and I encourage you to take the first step. Our hope is that you will not only change your own life, but also open the door for other people to change theirs.

TIM & TREY

In this six-week study, we will encourage you—from our own experience—to form intentional relationships with people who are different from you. In the process, you will discover the power of unlikely friendships—friendships that can transform your life, your community, and maybe even the world. Whether the lines of division in your life are racial, religious, ideological, or even something as simple as a difference in age or experience, we will show you how to pursue reconciliation by learning how to listen to, understand, and build rapport with people who at first may seem to have little in common with you.

This workbook is designed for both personal and group study. To get the most out of your small group meetings, we suggest that all members work through the chapters on their own each week before coming together for discussion with the group. We have intentionally packed a lot into each session, to encourage your engagement with and reflection on the topics of friendship and reconciliation. Group leaders and members can decide which questions (and how many) to discuss in each session, depending on the length of your meeting and the composition of your group.

We encourage you to identify someone—whether it is a person or a group—with whom you'd like to develop an intentional friendship across a line of division in your life. Invite that person or group to join you in this study and learn how to leverage the power of unlikely friendships to create a better community, a better nation, and a better world. By taking the important first step—initiating a dialogue—you can be part of the solution to the all-too-common problems of separation and division.

Why Reconciliation?

The Power of Unlikely Friendships

WATCH

To watch the introductory video (3–5 minutes) for session 1, go to the Why Reconciliation? link at www.thefriendship challenge.com.

CONSIDER

Many Americans say they feel disconnected from one another. Why? We are really good at rattling off our differences: liberal or conservative; millennial or baby boomer; black, white, or brown; Catholic or Protestant; Muslim or Christian; one-percenter, middle-class, or poor; Northern or Southern; and the list goes on. In many ways, we are polarized and divided as a nation. But what about our similarities? Can we list those as quickly and easily? How about some of these:

We all want what's best for our children.

We all want to live in a safe and peaceful community.

We all want opportunities for meaningful work that allows us to provide for our families.

We all want to enjoy a nice meal with good company.

We all want a secure future for ourselves, our children, and our parents.

If we think about it, don't we have a lot more in common with other people than we may have realized? Aren't there more things—and more important things—that unite us than separate us? And how many of the things that separate us are the result of different perspectives about how to reach the same goals?

What if, instead of focusing on our differences, we focused on everything we have in common with other people? What if we pursued intentional relationships across lines of division with the goal of reconciliation? What if we formed genuine friendships based on mutual understanding and respect? The point is not to erase our differences—in a pluralistic society, our diversity makes us who we are—but to make an intentional decision to listen, learn, seek understanding, find points of agreement, and disagree with civility and grace. The road to reconciliation begins with a simple choice to invite someone with whom we differ to have a conversation.

REFLECT

1. When have you witnessed the power of a friendship or a relationship to change things for the better—in your family, neighborhood, or community?

2. Think of someone who, at least on the surface, seems totally opposite from you. It may be someone who has opposing views or a different life experience. What makes you different from each other?

   Now describe some of the similarities you have with this same person.

   How does identifying your similarities affect your perspective on your differences?

DIG DEEPER

1. As you read the following passage, look for differences between Jesus and the woman at the well.

Jesus knew the Pharisees had heard that he was baptizing and making more disciples than John (though Jesus himself didn't baptize them—his disciples did). So he left Judea and returned to Galilee.

He had to go through Samaria on the way. Eventually he came to the Samaritan village of Sychar, near the field that Jacob gave to his son Joseph. Jacob's well was there; and Jesus, tired from the long walk, sat wearily beside the well about noontime. Soon a Samaritan woman came to draw water, and Jesus said to her, "Please give me a drink." He was alone at the time because his disciples had gone into the village to buy some food.

The woman was surprised, for Jews refuse to have anything to do with Samaritans. She said to Jesus, "You are a Jew, and I am a Samaritan woman. Why are you asking me for a drink?"

Jesus replied, "If you only knew the gift God has for you and who you are speaking to, you would ask me, and I would give you living water."

"But sir, you don't have a rope or a bucket," she said, "and this well is very deep. Where would you get this living water? And besides, do you think you're greater than our ancestor Jacob, who gave us this well? How can you offer better water than he and his sons and his animals enjoyed?"

Jesus replied, "Anyone who drinks this water will soon become thirsty again. But those who drink the water I give will never be thirsty again. It becomes a fresh, bubbling spring within them, giving them eternal life."

"Please, sir," the woman said, "give me this water! Then I'll never be thirsty again, and I won't have to come here to get water."

"Go and get your husband," Jesus told her.

"I don't have a husband," the woman replied.

Jesus said, "You're right! You don't have a husband—for you have had five husbands, and you aren't even married to the man you're living with now. You certainly spoke the truth!"

"Sir," the woman said, "you must be a prophet. So tell me, why is it that you Jews insist that Jerusalem is the only place of worship, while we Samaritans claim it is here at Mount Gerizim, where our ancestors worshiped?"

Jesus replied, "Believe me, dear woman, the time is coming when it will no longer matter whether you worship the Father on this mountain or in Jerusalem. You Samaritans know very little about the one you worship, while we Jews know all about him, for salvation comes through the Jews. But the time is coming—indeed it's here now—when true worshipers will worship the Father in spirit and in truth. The Father is looking for those who will worship him that way. For God is Spirit, so those who worship him must worship in spirit and in truth."

The woman said, "I know the Messiah is coming—the one who is called Christ. When he comes, he will explain everything to us."

Then Jesus told her, "I Am the Messiah!"

JOHN 4:1-26

a. List at least three differences Jesus had with the woman at the well.

b. How does the woman use these differences to try to avoid Jesus' request for water?

c. What reasons do *you* use for trying to avoid connecting with others who are different from you?

2. Read the next part of the passage:

Just then his disciples came back. They were shocked
to find him talking to a woman, but none of them
had the nerve to ask, "What do you want with her?"
or "Why are you talking to her?" The woman left her
water jar beside the well and ran back to the village,
telling everyone, "Come and see a man who told
me everything I ever did! Could he possibly be the
Messiah?" So the people came streaming from the
village to see him.

Meanwhile, the disciples were urging Jesus,
"Rabbi, eat something."

But Jesus replied, "I have a kind of food you
know nothing about."

"Did someone bring him food while we were
gone?" the disciples asked each other.

Then Jesus explained: "My nourishment comes
from doing the will of God, who sent me, and from
finishing his work. You know the saying, 'Four
months between planting and harvest.' But I say,
wake up and look around. The fields are already
ripe for harvest. The harvesters are paid good
wages, and the fruit they harvest is people brought
to eternal life. What joy awaits both the planter
and the harvester alike! You know the saying, 'One
plants and another harvests.' And it's true. I sent
you to harvest where you didn't plant; others had

already done the work, and now you will get to
gather the harvest."

JOHN 4:27-38

a. Why were the disciples surprised to find Jesus talking
to the woman?

b. Even though the disciples had witnessed Jesus' work
and mission firsthand, they were still shocked by his
actions. Why do you think this is?

c. Complete the following sentence with the name
of someone with whom you differ: *My friends or
family members would be surprised to see me having
a conversation with* _____. Why would
they be surprised?

d. What is the "nourishment" that Jesus speaks of here? What does he say is the source of this nourishment?

e. Can you say that your own nourishment comes from the same source? Why or why not?

f. If the "fruit" of the harvest is "people brought to eternal life," what opportunities might we be missing if we do not have relationships with people who are different from us?

3. Read the final portion of the passage:

Many Samaritans from the village believed in Jesus because the woman had said, "He told me everything I ever did!" When they came out to see him, they begged him to stay in their village. So he stayed for two days, long enough for many more to hear his message and believe. Then they said

to the woman, "Now we believe, not just because
of what you told us, but because we have heard
him ourselves. Now we know that he is indeed
the Savior of the world."

JOHN 4:39-42

a. Based on these verses, how were the Samaritan
   people affected by Jesus' encounter with the woman
   at the well?

b. What kind of impact could you have on the people
   around you by starting a relationship with someone
   who is different?

c. Are you ready to reach across lines of division in
   your life to connect with someone who is different?
   Explain why or why not, including any hesitations
   or challenges you may have.

RESPOND

1. As Christians, we believe that Jesus reconciles sinners to a sinless God. Moreover, in order to reconcile us to God, Jesus crossed many lines of division. Though he was the Son of God, he was born into this world to an unwed mother, grew up in meager economic circumstances, and had no settled home as an adult. Though he invested his life in helping other people—teaching them the truth about God and about salvation, healing the sick, casting out demons, and restoring people's lives—he was arrested on phony charges, tried before a biased tribunal, and put to death for crimes he did not commit. Even as he was being executed on a cross between two thieves, he cried out to God to forgive the very people who were killing him. His willingness to forgive even the worst of sinners is the foundation for our willingness to be reconciled to one another—even to those who are very different from us, and to those who may even be opposed to us. Jesus' example of sacrificial love is what enables us to offer grace, extend forgiveness, seek understanding, and pursue reconciliation.

   a. How does this perspective affect your decision to initiate a relationship with someone who is different from you?

b. Are there any people in your life who are off-limits? Explain.

2. One of the keys to overcoming problems in our society is finding common ground. We don't have to agree on *everything*, but wherever we *do* agree . . . let's start there. I (Tim) have found commonality to be a powerful tool. Trey understands the concept of mutually beneficial opportunities as well as anyone I have ever met, especially in leadership. His lifestyle reflects what we're talking about. One of the reasons Trey and I have been able to have some frank discussions about problems, challenges, and obstacles—and overcome them very quickly—is that we have intentionally sought to find common ground. No matter what differences we may have with another person—social, racial, political, spiritual, ideological—if we will look for *something* we have in common, or something we can admire or emulate in the other person, we can always build on that.[2]

a. Do you agree or disagree that there is always something we have in common with other people that we can build on? Explain.

b. Why do you think it is sometimes easier to focus on our differences than on what we have in common?

c. Think specifically about the person or group with whom you most need to reconcile. How can starting with common ground open a pathway for frank discussions about problems, challenges, and obstacles?

3. In *Unified*, we discuss our different perspectives on the shootings at Emanuel AME Church in Charleston. Do you recall your first thoughts when you heard about the tragedy? Did you talk about it with anyone? Did the shootings affect you in any way? Why or why not?

4. In Washington, on the day after the shootings, there was a massive prayer vigil on the Capitol grounds. People of every background and political persuasion gathered to pray. It was beautiful and compelling to

see the emotional boundaries lifted, to see people come together to comfort one another. It reminded me (Trey) of all that is *good* about America. But why does it take a tragedy for us to come together so beautifully? Why must we face a calamity before we will join hands, pray, and seek healing?[3]

Discuss your responses to these two questions.

5. I (Tim) have always been impressed by what I call the "aftermath mentality." As Americans, we are so good at treating each other as individuals and family *after* a crisis. Think about 9/11. Think about hurricanes and other natural disasters. It is amazing to see how people will pull together to help, across all barriers and boundaries, when something bad happens. But I would like to see us develop an aftermath mentality *without* the crisis. Maybe we can avoid a future tragedy if we will act like the American family we are without waiting for an *event* to ignite that response.[4]

What steps can we take to develop an "aftermath mentality" *before* there is another crisis?

6. How do suffering and tragedy affect our willingness and ability to pursue reconciliation? Do they help or hurt? Explain.

7. How does the kind of forgiveness modeled by the families of the victims of the Charleston shootings factor into reconciliation? What or who needs to be forgiven, corporately or individually, as part of your effort to pursue reconciliation with someone with whom you have differences? In other words, is anything blocking you from pursuing a relationship with someone in the "other camp"?

RECONCILIATION IN ACTION

1. What are some of your own prejudices or fears that you may need to confront and overcome in order to pursue a relationship with someone who is different from you?

2. What steps can you take to start a relationship across a line of separation in your life—an intentional relationship trending toward reconciliation? What are some of the challenges you may face? Who can help you overcome these challenges?

3. Set a date to attend an event that will help you connect and explore reconciliation with someone who is different from you. This is only a first step. You simply want to get out and see how it feels to be with someone from your "other" group as you work to develop further steps to build bridges and find common ground. How could attending a church service or a social function with someone across a line of division help you both begin to reconcile your differences?

4. After the event, write down how you felt. Were you surprised by the meeting? Did you feel awkward, or were you comfortable? How did the person or group receive you? What things did you discover you had in common?

Creating Rapport

Connect on What You Have in Common

WATCH

To watch the introductory video (3–5 minutes) for session 2, go to the Creating Rapport link at www.thefriendship challenge.com.

CONSIDER

Our friendship began when we were both elected to Congress from South Carolina. Along with fellow freshmen Jeff Duncan and Mick Mulvaney, we met to discuss our common interests, confer on the issues, and discuss upcoming votes. We ate dinner together as often as we could, using each other as sounding boards to take advantage of our different perspectives and passions and our varying levels of experience and expertise. Through times of testing and as we worked together to represent the people of our state, we began to establish rapport with one another.

Building rapport is the first step toward genuine reconciliation. You can establish rapport by focusing on what you already have in common with the other person. If you will sit down with someone long enough to find a common connection, we think you'll find you have most things in common with most people.

As you seek to build rapport and trust with someone, you must be willing to see the world from a perspective that is not your own. It's amazing how much you can learn if you will humbly engage in conversation with someone, be willing to listen, and seek to understand.

It's important that we understand our differences, but if we want to build friendships with people across lines of division, we must focus on what we have in common and not become distracted by what separates us. We do this naturally—and often without even thinking about it—when we feel a connection with someone. If we want to reach out to people who are different from us, the process is really the same—though we may need to be more *intentional* about it. We must start by establishing rapport, based on common interests, and build a foundation of trust and goodwill, before we gravitate toward conversations about problems and the issues that divide us. If we start by talking about the things we can agree on, eventually we will pave the way to more challenging and difficult conversations. It won't happen overnight, and it may not happen the way we expect, or with whom we expect. But if we can establish rapport, we will be one step closer to reconciliation and understanding.[5]

REFLECT

1. How can having a good rapport help when misunderstanding or conflict arises—such as when someone says or does something you find offensive?

2. Identify a person or group with whom you're interested in developing a friendship to work toward reconciliation. What things do you already know you have in common? Describe what else you already know about this person or group.

3. To build on a positive foundation, what do you admire about this person or group?

4. Do you think this person or group will be amenable to developing rapport with you? Why or why not? What can you do to overcome barriers to building rapport?

5. What activities can you do together as you seek to develop rapport?

DIG DEEPER

The Bible gives us several examples of friendships that formed despite people's differences. As you read the following passages about David and Jonathan, Saul and Ananias, and Solomon and the queen of Sheba, look for ways in which the two parties developed rapport. Underline words that show how they developed a bond.

1. Consider the story of David and Jonathan:

After David had finished talking with Saul, he met Jonathan, the king's son. There was an immediate bond between them, for Jonathan loved David. From that day on Saul kept David with him and wouldn't let him return home. And Jonathan made a solemn pact with David, because he loved him as he loved himself. Jonathan sealed the pact by taking off his robe and giving it to David, together with his tunic, sword, bow, and belt.

1 SAMUEL 18:1-4

a. Jonathan was the eldest son of King Saul, making him heir to the throne. David was the son of a common shepherd named Jesse. Jonathan grew up in the king's household. David grew up tending sheep out in the fields. Though these two young men were different in many ways, they established "an immediate bond" when they met. What do you think made this bond possible?

b. Besides their differences in background, what other challenges to friendship did they have to overcome? (See 1 Samuel 18:7-8; 20:30-31.)

2. The apostle Paul started off as Saul, a man who
   vehemently persecuted God's people. Read the
   passage below about Saul's conversion and
   the man who reached across boundaries to
   help him. Look for the ways in which they
   developed rapport.

Saul was uttering threats with every breath and
was eager to kill the Lord's followers. So he went
to the high priest. He requested letters addressed
to the synagogues in Damascus, asking for their
cooperation in the arrest of any followers of the
Way he found there. He wanted to bring them—
both men and women—back to Jerusalem in
chains.

As he was approaching Damascus on this
mission, a light from heaven suddenly shone down
around him. He fell to the ground and heard a
voice saying to him, "Saul! Saul! Why are you
persecuting me?"

"Who are you, lord?" Saul asked.

And the voice replied, "I am Jesus, the one you
are persecuting! Now get up and go into the city, and
you will be told what you must do."

The men with Saul stood speechless, for they
heard the sound of someone's voice but saw no one!
Saul picked himself up off the ground, but when he
opened his eyes he was blind. So his companions led

him by the hand to Damascus. He remained there blind for three days and did not eat or drink.

Now there was a believer in Damascus named Ananias. The Lord spoke to him in a vision, calling, "Ananias!"

"Yes, Lord!" he replied.

The Lord said, "Go over to Straight Street, to the house of Judas. When you get there, ask for a man from Tarsus named Saul. He is praying to me right now. I have shown him a vision of a man named Ananias coming in and laying hands on him so he can see again."

"But Lord," exclaimed Ananias, "I've heard many people talk about the terrible things this man has done to the believers in Jerusalem! And he is authorized by the leading priests to arrest everyone who calls upon your name."

But the Lord said, "Go, for Saul is my chosen instrument to take my message to the Gentiles and to kings, as well as to the people of Israel. And I will show him how much he must suffer for my name's sake."

So Ananias went and found Saul. He laid his hands on him and said, "Brother Saul, the Lord Jesus, who appeared to you on the road, has sent me so that you might regain your sight and be filled with the Holy Spirit." Instantly something like scales fell from Saul's eyes, and he regained his sight. Then

he got up and was baptized. Afterward he ate some
food and regained his strength.

ACTS 9:1-19

a. Why did Ananias reach out to Saul?

b. What did God tell Ananias that Saul was chosen
to do?

c. What apprehensions did Ananias have about
crossing boundaries to help Saul?

3. Read the story of Solomon and the queen of Sheba:

When the queen of Sheba heard of Solomon's fame,
which brought honor to the name of the LORD, she
came to test him with hard questions. She arrived
in Jerusalem with a large group of attendants and
a great caravan of camels loaded with spices, large

quantities of gold, and precious jewels. When she met with Solomon, she talked with him about everything she had on her mind. Solomon had answers for all her questions; nothing was too hard for the king to explain to her. When the queen of Sheba realized how very wise Solomon was, and when she saw the palace he had built, she was overwhelmed. She was also amazed at the food on his tables, the organization of his officials and their splendid clothing, the cup-bearers, and the burnt offerings Solomon made at the Temple of the LORD.

She exclaimed to the king, "Everything I heard in my country about your achievements and wisdom is true! I didn't believe what was said until I arrived here and saw it with my own eyes. In fact, I had not heard the half of it! Your wisdom and prosperity are far beyond what I was told. How happy your people must be! What a privilege for your officials to stand here day after day, listening to your wisdom! Praise the LORD your God, who delights in you and has placed you on the throne of Israel. Because of the LORD's eternal love for Israel, he has made you king so you can rule with justice and righteousness."

Then she gave the king a gift of 9,000 pounds of gold, great quantities of spices, and precious jewels. Never again were so many spices brought in as those the queen of Sheba gave to King Solomon.

I KINGS 10:1-10

    a. What presuppositions (positive or negative) did the queen of Sheba have about Solomon?

    b. How did the queen of Sheba develop rapport with Solomon?

RESPOND

1. For me (Trey), our friendship took a dramatic turn one evening when Tim showed up to the table looking overwhelmed and perplexed, which was odd. I'd never seen him anything less than fully composed and fully in control. When I asked if there was anything I could do, anything he needed, he shared with me the darker side of being politically sought after. Turned out, there actually were some frustrations with living in the spotlight, being everything the rest of the world wanted him to be. Tim was famous, in demand, constantly sought out. He was also exhausted—both physically and emotionally.

    As he still does at times today, he was trying to say yes to everyone and everything, and he was being pulled in a thousand directions. Colleagues were asking

him to get involved in nearly every major legis
initiative, and he was struggling to say no. On the
night, and for just a moment, he seemed vulnerable.
He seemed mortal. He seemed to be in need of some
trusted counsel and a friend who would simply listen.[6]

a. What is the value of vulnerability in building
rapport? What are some barriers to honesty and
vulnerability in a relationship? How can we
overcome those?

b. Discuss the importance of listening in building
rapport. How do you know when to offer advice
and when to just listen?

c. In our culture, showing vulnerability is often
perceived as a weakness. In what ways can it actually
be a strength? What practical steps can we take in
our relationships to create a "safe space" for honesty
and vulnerability?

2. In so many ways, Trey and I are two very different people. I'm a big-picture person, and I like to focus on vision. Trey is more analytical and strategic. He remembers everything that ever happened. Others have told me my memory is very good, but I don't necessarily agree. I try to have a *selective* memory: I choose not to remember the negative. It's actually a pretty effective strategy. I lead with hope; Trey is more of a skeptic. He thinks well on his feet and is an expert at cross-examination; I tend to analyze things later. He's a fantastic student, and his preparation is impeccable. I enjoy assessing and planning, but he enjoys dissecting. I've worked hard to excel, but Trey is naturally brilliant. Because of our different backgrounds and life experiences, there are times when our vantage points are polar opposites. But one thing that binds us together is a true desire to know each other beyond our differences. We utilize that knowledge and our different perspectives to make each other better.[7]

a. What differences do you have with your unlikely friend(s) that might actually be strengths? How do your differing perspectives make the other person better?

b. Romans 12:10 says, "Love each other with genuine affection, and take delight in honoring each other." How can you apply this verse to the unlikely friendship(s) you are building? Be specific.

RECONCILIATION IN ACTION

1. Have you met at least once with the person or group with whom you are seeking to build a relationship? How did the meeting go? When are you meeting again?

2. Based on your conversation with the person you are getting to know, describe what you now know about him or her. How can this information help you build rapport? Here are some questions to help you get started:

   • What do you admire about this person?
   • What do you both like or enjoy?
   • How does this person affect the people around him or her?

- What struggles has he or she overcome?
- What are some of his or her biggest achievements?
- What was your strongest point of connection or understanding?

3. Write a note to your new friend and share what you see in him or her that makes you want to continue working toward reconciliation and bridge building.

Establishing Credibility

Begin to Trust

WATCH

To watch the introductory video (3–5 minutes) for session 3, go to the Establishing Credibility link at www.thefriendship challenge.com.

CONSIDER

We establish credibility with others by being honest, genuine, and transparent in our communication. If we're honest about where we're coming from, we can often bridge the gap between our differences by increasing our understanding. The more we understand each other, the easier it is to build trust. Credibility is also built on *commitment*—when we're willing to say to the other person, "I'm in your corner, no matter what." That doesn't happen overnight. It takes purpose, patience, and persistence.

Before we can address the issues that divide us, we must first establish credibility in those areas. In politics and in life, we create credibility by doing our homework and becoming proficient on a topic. In a relationship, credibility is born from our desire to know more about the other person. When we are genuinely interested in understanding other people's perspectives, we will find ourselves able to move quickly and more deeply into relationships with them. In a group, rapport is established through common bonds and core values. These allow for credibility to grow quickly, leading to deeper friendships.

Sometimes our history seems much more powerful than our present circumstances. Ordinarily, having a good memory is a positive thing. But it doesn't necessarily help when we're trying to clear a path toward reconciliation. Memory can become a burden when we can so easily remember the bad things that have happened, the ways in which we have felt wronged, or the ways we have suffered. Having a short memory with the challenges of the past can serve us well because it allows us to get on to the next opportunity. That isn't to say we forget about the past, but we learn from it and keep moving forward. In order to focus on the bridges we're trying to build, we must be willing to forgive what others have done—or not done.

One important step toward understanding and reconciliation involves what we call *cleaning the slate*—choosing to wipe away preconceived thoughts about a person or a group and agreeing to start fresh. Fresh starts are always challenging. New beginnings must be intentional and mutual. They require restraint, grace, and love. If we're going to move in the direction of reconciliation, we should not blame each other for what other people have done. Although it's impossible to forget the past, we can choose not to *dwell* on it. We can make a conscious and deliberate decision to forgive others and ourselves.

Cleaning the slate does not mean minimizing, excusing, or forgetting the past. Our history matters—both how we got here collectively as a nation, and how we move forward into the future—but when we clean the slate, we make a conscious decision to allow the past to remain in the past. We don't dredge it up and make it foundational in our present relationships. It isn't that we don't remember, but we choose not to allow the past to impinge on our present relationships.[8]

REFLECT

1. When have you experienced or witnessed a friendship built on credibility and trust?

2. What does it take for you to trust someone? What are the essential building blocks of trust?

3. How has trust (or the lack of trust) changed your relationships?

4. Have you been able to share a vulnerable part of your story or journey with someone who is different from you? What obstacles did you face?

5. Cleaning the slate can be one of the most difficult parts of working toward reconciliation. Often, the slate that most needs cleaning is the one inside each of us. Starting with a good, long look in the mirror, what preconceptions, prejudices, and negative attitudes do you need to take responsibility for before you can clean the slate and begin to trust someone else?

6. Now that you have cleaned your own slate—what the Bible calls removing the plank from your own eye—what obstacles remain that would make it difficult to clean the slate with another person?

DIG DEEPER

1. Recognizing that some parts of history are easier to reconcile than others, use the following Scripture passage to explore the concept of creating a clean slate:

Peter came to him and asked, "Lord, how often should I forgive someone who sins against me? Seven times?"

"No, not seven times," Jesus replied, "but seventy times seven!

"Therefore, the Kingdom of Heaven can be compared to a king who decided to bring his accounts up to date with servants who had borrowed money from him. In the process, one of his debtors was brought in who owed him millions of dollars. He couldn't pay, so his master ordered that he be sold—along with his wife, his children, and everything he owned—to pay the debt.

"But the man fell down before his master and begged him, 'Please, be patient with me, and I will pay it all.' Then his master was filled with pity for him, and he released him and forgave his debt.

"But when the man left the king, he went to a fellow servant who owed him a few thousand dollars. He grabbed him by the throat and demanded instant payment.

"His fellow servant fell down before him and begged for a little more time. 'Be patient with me, and I will pay it,' he pleaded. But his creditor wouldn't wait. He had the man arrested and put in prison until the debt could be paid in full.

"When some of the other servants saw this, they were very upset. They went to the king and told him everything that had happened. Then the king called in the man he had forgiven and said, 'You evil servant! I forgave you that tremendous debt because you pleaded with me. Shouldn't you have mercy on your fellow servant, just as I had mercy on you?' Then the angry king sent the man to prison to be tortured until he had paid his entire debt.

"That's what my heavenly Father will do to you if you refuse to forgive your brothers and sisters from your heart."

MATTHEW 18:21-35

a. How does the parable of the unforgiving debtor apply to the challenge of cleaning the slate in your relationships?

b. When it seems difficult not to allow the past to impinge on the present, how can this passage help you to forgive?

c. How can we avoid being like the servant who wouldn't forgive the debt?

d. What is the relationship between justice, forgiveness, and mercy?

2. Whether we realize it or not, we tend to impute characteristics to other people, and we view them

through the prism of our past relationships. It's hard work to resist the temptation to see a person as part of a group, or as a "type," rather than as an individual. It takes serious effort to be aware of our attitudes and prejudices, and to give people the benefit of the doubt. But dealing with people as individuals is absolutely essential for overcoming stereotypes. Reconciliation requires relationship, and relationship requires fairness and self-awareness.[9]

a. When dealing with someone who is different from you, do you tend to see that person as an individual or as a member of a group? Explain.

b. How has developing a relationship with someone who is different from you challenged your prejudices or preconceived notions?

c. What practical steps can you take to see individuals rather than groups?

1. Prejudice has to do with a lot more than skin color. It can be about any line of division in our lives—age, culture, social status, religion, ideology. Before we can solve a problem, we must first identify it and face it. Think of a time when you allowed prejudice to cloud your judgment about others. What was it that allowed you to look beyond your initial impressions or preconceived ideas to see that person or group from a new perspective? How can you apply what you've learned to overcome prejudice in other areas as well?

RECONCILIATION IN ACTION

Have you met at least once with the person or group with whom you are seeking to build a relationship? Keep track of how your relationship is developing and how you are changing as a result.

1. What has changed in how you perceive the person or group you are learning more about?

2. Are you building trust and establishing credibility? Why or why not?

3. What one activity do you enjoy together? How can you schedule more time to participate in it?

4. What roadblocks have you encountered to developing credibility and trust? How can you overcome these challenges in this relationship (or perhaps in future relationships)?

5. What concerns do you still have about reconciliation?

Problem-Solving

Agree on What's Missing the Mark

WATCH

To watch the introductory video (3–5 minutes) for session 4, go to the Problem-Solving link at www.thefriendship challenge.com.

CONSIDER

Once we have established rapport, trust, and credibility with someone, we may be ready to enter into deeper conversations—to discuss the challenges we face and tackle some of our differences. Trust allows us to identify problems from a common perspective, walk through those problems together, and begin to look for mutually beneficial solutions. The process of building rapport and credibility gives us the understanding of each other we need to work constructively together in an atmosphere of trust and goodwill.

So often, it seems, we look for solutions the wrong way. We put the cart before the horse and try to solve problems that we haven't yet agreed we both have. We can't begin to solve our problems until we've established a common bond and desire to work together. Effective problem-solving can only happen when we've taken the time and put in the effort to establish a genuine and positive working relationship.[10]

Problem-solving across lines of division requires *intentionality*. If we are intentional in our desire for a relationship to grow, and we will make time for it, we can accomplish a lot with people with whom we might otherwise think we have little in common. Unlikely friendships don't just happen. We have to make it a priority to pursue friendships with people who are different from us.

One way to tell that you're in an unlikely friendship is when your other friends start taking notice and asking questions.

"I'm surprised to see you with so-and-so."

"Why are you talking with her?"

"Why are you meeting with him?"

Those questions can open the door for long and deep conversations with friends with whom you may have more in common. It could be a perfect opportunity to share what you have learned about uncommon friendships and to invite your old friends to get to know your new friends. In other words, you can become a bridge of reconciliation between people who might otherwise never interact with one another.

To overcome the challenges we face in our communities and in our world, it helps if we start by establishing common ground. Common goals and values can become a catalyst for solving problems and overcoming challenges.

REFLECT

1. How has a positive friendship with someone you once thought was so different affected you or your family?

2. Has your unlikely friendship prompted others to ask about your differences? How have you responded?

3. Do you feel comfortable introducing your new friends to other people in your life who may identify more closely with you? Why or why not?

4. What do you want to change in your community? How can you begin to discuss this issue with an unlikely friend? What boundaries will you need to set for the conversation? Can you agree to respect each other's views as you venture into deeper discussions?

DIG DEEPER

1. Read the following passage and note the differences between Rahab and the Israelites.

Joshua secretly sent out two spies from the Israelite camp at Acacia Grove. He instructed them, "Scout out the land on the other side of the Jordan River, especially around Jericho." So the two men set out and came to the house of a prostitute named Rahab and stayed there that night.

But someone told the king of Jericho, "Some Israelites have come here tonight to spy out the land." So the king of Jericho sent orders to Rahab: "Bring out the men who have come into your house, for they have come here to spy out the whole land."

Rahab had hidden the two men, but she replied, "Yes, the men were here earlier, but I didn't know where they were from. They left the town at dusk, as the gates were about to close. I don't know where they went. If you hurry, you can probably catch up with them." (Actually, she had taken them up to the roof and hidden them beneath bundles of flax she had laid out.) So the king's men went looking for the spies along the road leading to the shallow crossings of the Jordan River. And as soon as the king's men had left, the gate of Jericho was shut.

Before the spies went to sleep that night, Rahab went up on the roof to talk with them. "I know the LORD has given you this land," she told them. "We are all afraid of you. Everyone in the land is living in terror. For we have heard how the LORD made a dry path for you through the Red Sea when you left Egypt. And we know what you did to Sihon and Og, the two Amorite kings east of the Jordan River, whose people you completely destroyed. No wonder our hearts have melted in fear! No one has the courage to fight after hearing such things. For the LORD your God is the supreme God of the heavens above and the earth below.

"Now swear to me by the LORD that you will be kind to me and my family since I have helped you. Give me some guarantee that when Jericho is conquered, you will let me live, along with my father and mother, my brothers and sisters, and all their families."

"We offer our own lives as a guarantee for your safety," the men agreed. "If you don't betray us, we will keep our promise and be kind to you when the LORD gives us the land."

Then, since Rahab's house was built into the town wall, she let them down by a rope through the window. "Escape to the hill country," she told them. "Hide there for three days from the men searching for you. Then, when they have returned, you can go on your way."

Before they left, the men told her, "We will be bound by the oath we have taken only if you follow these instructions. When we come into the land, you must leave this scarlet rope hanging from the window through which you let us down. And all your family members—your father, mother, brothers, and all your relatives—must be here inside the house. If they go out into the street and are killed, it will not be our fault. But if anyone lays a hand on people inside this house, we will accept the responsibility for their death. If you betray us, however, we are not bound by this oath in any way."

"I accept your terms," she replied. And she sent them on their way, leaving the scarlet rope hanging from the window.

The spies went up into the hill country and stayed there three days. The men who were chasing them searched everywhere along the road, but they finally returned without success.

Then the two spies came down from the hill country, crossed the Jordan River, and reported to Joshua all that had happened to them. "The LORD has given us the whole land," they said, "for all the people in the land are terrified of us."

JOSHUA 2:1-24

a. List three differences between Rahab and the Israelites.

(1)

(2)

(3)

b. What problem did Rahab help the Israelites solve?

c. How did the Israelites in turn help Rahab?

d. Why did Rahab help the Israelites?

e. Why do you think she trusted the spies enough to help them?

f. Why do you think the spies trusted Rahab?

g. What can you learn from this story to help you develop friendships across lines of division?

RESPOND

In 2016, Tim and I began hosting Pastor/Police Roundtables throughout South Carolina, bringing together pastors, law enforcement officers, and administrators. Our mission was to learn about community relations, interactions between the community and law enforcement, and the similarities and differences among blacks and whites regarding their views of the criminal justice system. Our goal was to provide a safe environment to listen, to vent, to express anger, and to express hope.

We wanted to create a place where real people could express real emotions and do so with an eye toward remedy, understanding, and conciliation. We wanted to cultivate an environment where women and men with a common purpose could meet one another, eat together, talk with honesty, laugh with openness, and disagree with clarity and safety. Still, we were not naive. We know that change doesn't happen overnight or over lunch. But the *desire* for change can happen overnight, and our goal was to establish rapport and create that environment to plant the seeds of trust and credibility.

The Pastor/Police Roundtables have proved to be a great way to initiate open and honest conversations between church leaders and law enforcement. This same format could be used to foster communication between people of any opposing sides—police and pastors; Republicans and Democrats; Muslims and Christians; or people with differing views on the death penalty, health care, term limits, the national deficit, or any other issue with the potential to divide us. The possible lines of conflict in our country seem endless. But the opportunities for dialogue and understanding truly *are* endless. Reconciliation can begin with one conversation and one friendship, and it can cross any barrier in existence.[11]

1. What advantages might there be in discussing issues with people who have similar or different perspectives?

2. What unique forums are available to you to foster discussions between people who have differences with each other? What would it take to get something started?

3. What are some guidelines you'll want to establish before initiating these discussions?

4. Even if your roundtable discussions do not result in ultimate solutions, what other outcomes would you consider to be a win? (For example: decreasing the intensity of emotions around the subject of discussion.)

5. How can sharing a meal together help to foster discussion between people with differences?

6. When was the last time you had a person from a different race, a different culture, or a different background from yours into your home for a meal? Who can you invite—and how soon?

RECONCILIATION IN ACTION

1. As you continue to build trust and credibility in your new friendships, what issues would you like to address?

2. Set a time to have a conversation about an issue that is important to both of you. Establish guidelines and develop goals with the other person/people before you begin. Use the space below to record your thoughts and emotions about the experience immediately afterward.

3. What did you learn through the process?

4. What projects can you work on together to increase awareness of the issue under discussion? Choose one project and agree together on how and when to do it.

Building Bridges

Toward a Brighter Future

WATCH

To watch the introductory video (3–5 minutes) for session 5, go to the Building Bridges link at www.thefriendship challenge.com.

CONSIDER

If you will seek to establish an unlikely friendship with someone who differs from you, we promise you that one of two things will happen. Either you will see things from a new perspective that you've never considered before, and you will be changed; or you will become even more convinced, after careful reflection, that your approach is right and proper. Either way, you win.

Even if you decide that your own beliefs are correct, that doesn't necessarily make the other person wrong. Once you've seen life through a different set of lenses, you'll understand better how a person of good conscience could reach conclusions different from your own. And maybe—just maybe—you'll find a way to move forward together, building bridges of cooperation and understanding as you pursue mutually beneficial outcomes. You have nothing to lose by trying.

We're not going to solve the great complexities of life the first time we meet someone. But we can start building a foundation by listening. We can start by trying to understand. It may not feel natural at first, and it may even be terribly awkward. But try reaching out to someone who does not expect it. Simply say, "I'd like to have a conversation. I'd like to get to know you, and I'd like to understand your perspective. I'll let you choose what we'll talk about. We're not going to argue, we won't correct each other, we won't rebuke each other, and we won't try to talk over one another. My main purpose will be to listen. And let's see where we go from there."[12]

How can we change the world? One relationship at a time. We'll do it by stepping out of our comfort zones and establishing friendships across lines of division. By focusing more on what we have in common than on what separates us, and by seeking out other people of good conscience, we can work together to achieve mutually beneficial outcomes.

It will take hard work. It will take intentionality. It will involve moving past what is familiar and comfortable, and learning how to establish rapport, credibility, and trust. It will mean reaching out to people we might otherwise never befriend. It will entail taking some risks to initiate deep conversations, share our thoughts and views, and seek ways to build bridges toward a brighter future.

REFLECT

1. What does a brighter future mean to you? Describe the beneficial outcomes you now foresee based on the issues you have explored during this study.

2. What positive changes do you envision for your neighborhood, your church, or your community?

3. How can your unlikely friendships help to build that bridge?

DIG DEEPER

1. Don't just pretend to love others. Really love them. Hate what is wrong. Hold tightly to what is good. Love each other with genuine affection, and take delight in honoring each other. Never be lazy, but work hard and serve the Lord enthusiastically. Rejoice in our confident hope. Be patient in trouble, and keep on praying. When God's people are in need, be ready to help them. Always be eager to practice hospitality.

   Bless those who persecute you. Don't curse them; pray that God will bless them. Be happy with those who are happy, and weep with those who weep. Live in harmony with each other. Don't be too proud to enjoy the company of ordinary people. And don't think you know it all!

   Never pay back evil with more evil. Do things in such a way that everyone can see you are honorable. Do all that you can to live in peace with everyone.

   Dear friends, never take revenge. Leave that to the righteous anger of God. For the Scriptures say,

   > "I will take revenge;
   >   I will pay them back,"
   >   says the Lord.

Instead,

> "If your enemies are hungry, feed them.
>   If they are thirsty, give them something to drink.
> In doing this, you will heap
>   burning coals of shame on their heads."

Don't let evil conquer you, but conquer evil by
doing good.

ROMANS 12:9-21

a. Which of these principles from Romans 12 are most
   applicable to your unlikely friendship? Which are the
   easiest or most difficult for you to do? Explain.

b. How can *listening* and *seeking to understand* help you
   put these principles into action?

RESPOND

Our opinions of law enforcement are grounded in our experiences, which affect how we see things. Read the following
perspectives and compare them with your own experience.

I (Tim) have lived in some very poor areas where crime

was rampant, and whenever the police patrolled our area or responded to a situation in the neighborhood, we were grateful. The situation was defused, and the officers were applauded. I remember distinctly the good officers who came to our aid when someone broke into my childhood home. My interactions with law enforcement have been positive and productive. The officers I've known are good people with a strong desire to serve justly. They want to do good, be good, and go home safe after a long shift.

There's no question that the African American community has a long and provocative history with law enforcement. This dates back to the earliest days of our nation, and we've seen a recent spike in aggressive interactions between law enforcement and people of color. We have experienced a level of turmoil not seen in decades, and my heart breaks for us all.

I, too, have had some difficult interactions, on both a personal and professional level. Most African Americans know the meaning of the initials DWB: Driving While Black. During one particular year in my time as an elected official, I was pulled over *seven* times. Was I speeding on one or two of those occasions? Most likely, yes. But the vast majority of times, I was pulled over for driving a new car in the wrong neighborhood, or for some other equally questionable reason. I'm all too familiar with the challenge of Driving While Black.

Police officers are a central part of our American family. Our nation is dependent on the rule of law, and we need honest, hardworking men and women to take up the shield. Police officers are men and women who see their job as a calling. They have two goals: to protect and serve. What will we do if they stop policing? Who will we call for help? We cannot allow the actions of a few to overwhelm the good of the majority, especially when so many do it so well. Let's focus on the fact that most law enforcement officers are true American heroes. It's hard to imagine putting your life on the line for people you've never met, yet they do it willingly, day in and day out. That's a ministry, actually. I like to think of police officers as ministers to society. It gives me great joy when I get to call someone in uniform with praise or congratulations. I am personally thankful for specific members of law enforcement who have been willing to stand with me during some very difficult times.

Yes, I have some questions and hesitations about decisions that a minority of law enforcement officers have made, but that is only part of the picture. I've been on enough ride-alongs to know the danger they face in their world, and I will never try to minimize that. It's precisely because I have so much respect for law enforcement as a whole that when they disappoint, especially when they misuse the authority of the badge, it is profoundly discouraging and frustrating. Along with that formal authority there must be a well-earned moral authority.[13]

Police officers are charged with maintaining law and order and protecting public safety. For me (Trey), as a former prosecutor, that means we preserve order, structure, stability, and security in our society by upholding the rule of law. But as I was preparing for a Pastor/Police Roundtable in Greenville, something told me that others might have a different understanding.

When I asked the participants what came to mind when they heard "law and order" and "public safety," a young black pastor was candid enough to speak up.

"I hear code talk," he said. "I hear, 'Lock up people of color' or 'Lock up young black males.'"

Wow. I appreciated his honesty, which got me thinking about the importance of defining our terms, being sensitive to what other people hear when we speak, and coming to a mutual understanding in our efforts to bridge the gap between what we say, what we mean, and what others think we mean when they hear our words.

When I use the phrase "law and order," I'm drawing a distinction between people of good conscience and people who are criminally inclined. It has nothing to do with race. It applies as equally to a middle-aged white male as it would to anyone else who breaks the law.

Every person of good conscience wants peace and security. To me, "law and order" does not mean "Let's lock 'em all up." It means "Let's keep everyone safe. Let's keep all people of good conscience safe."

When I speak, the intention behind my words is important; but what the other person *hears* is even more important. The quality of any communication is always determined by the listener. Unless the other person understands and receives what we meant to say, we haven't communicated effectively. We must speak the same language, define our terms, pursue a common understanding, and be bold and honest enough to speak up with one another, as that young pastor did with me. It doesn't have to be confrontational—in fact, it's better if it's not—but it must be candid, truthful, and to the point. And we must be willing to listen and seek to understand the other side's perspective.[14]

1. What did you learn from these two perspectives on law enforcement? Did anything surprise you? Explain.

2. How important do you think it is to *hear* what someone on the other side of an issue is saying?

3. How can you work with your unlikely friend(s) to develop your ability to hear other viewpoints?

RECONCILIATION IN ACTION

After you have developed a sufficient level of trust and rapport with your unlikely friend, sit down together to discuss an issue you see from different sides, using the following pointers to direct your conversation:

- Use articles, research, and firsthand experience to share your viewpoint on the issue. (Agree on an amount of time for this and set a timer.) Share *why* you feel the way you do.
- Ask your friend to share what he or she *heard* you say. Clarify any misunderstandings.
- Now repeat the exercise with your friend sharing his or her side of the issue through articles, research, and personal experience. Set a timer. Listen. Share what you *heard*. Seek clarification.

1. When you shared your perspective, did your friend hear you correctly? What misunderstandings arose? What did you learn about communicating your thoughts clearly?

2. When your friend shared his or her perspective, did you hear correctly? What misunderstandings arose? What did you learn about listening to other perspectives?

3. Did your viewpoint (and/or your friend's viewpoint) change as a result of the discussion? Why or why not?

4. Did you gain a better understanding of your friend's experience and perspective? Explain.

5. What other issues would you like to explore with your friend, or with others with whom you have differences?

Go Forth!

Live It Out

WATCH

To watch the introductory video (3–5 minutes) for session 6, go to the Go Forth! link at www.thefriendshipchallenge.com.

CONSIDER

We live in a world that prioritizes diversity over unity, but let's stop for a moment to recognize that those terms are not mutually exclusive. We can be unified *within* our diversity. We can allow our diversity to bring wisdom, texture, and depth to our unity. We have so much in common, and I (Trey) don't know why we don't spend at least as much time talking about our commonality as we do our differences.

We're all missing out on one of the greatest blessings of life if we don't pursue a friendship with someone who grew up differently from how we did, who doesn't look like us, who doesn't think like us, but who wants the same things from life that we do. All we have to do is just sit down and listen. Seek to understand a different perspective. Find points of agreement and harmony. Build rapport, credibility, and trust.[15]

How can we dream of a better way to live? How can we turn our dreams into reality? By taking one step at a time. Even if it's a bit uncomfortable at first. Realize that you may be doing something to change not only your own life but also someone else's.

I (Tim) have seen how unlikely friendships can create waves in our communities. When we're willing to reach across lines of division and focus on what we have in common, not on what separates us, our actions will affect people more than we realize. We need to decide what kind of positive waves we want our friendships to make.

For people of faith, prayer is always a good place to start. The Bible tells us that "the weapons we fight with are not the weapons of the world. On the contrary, they have divine power to demolish strongholds" (2 Corinthians 10:4, NIV). Prayer is certainly foremost among those weapons. Through prayer, we call on God to change people's hearts and minds—not so they'll agree with us, but so their intentions and actions will be brought into alignment with what *God* desires. We can pray the same for ourselves—and we should.

Trey and I are both optimistic and encouraged about the future of our country. Our optimism is rooted in our common faith in God and in his promise to guide us and sustain us as we trust in him. We're optimistic because we have seen so much good in people of diverse backgrounds. We have hope because we have seen a remarkable spirit of inclusiveness in the younger generations. Even though our nation may seem divided on the surface, we have confidence that we can get better as a people.

This is our vision for the future of America. We believe that our nation can be unified and transformed by conversations and friendships that lead to reconciliation and understanding.[16]

REFLECT

1. Describe the positive outcomes you would like to pursue through unlikely friendships.

2. Outline the steps you will take to turn your vision into reality.

3. With whom can you partner to pursue your vision for the future? What's the first step you can take to initiate a new friendship with this person or group?

DIG DEEPER

1. Read the following passages of Scripture and write in your own words what you think they say about the world you desire to live in.

Keep on loving each other as brothers and sisters. Don't forget to show hospitality to strangers, for some who have done this have entertained angels without realizing it! Remember those in prison, as if you were there yourself. Remember also those being mistreated, as if you felt their pain in your own bodies.

HEBREWS 13:1-3

Share each other's burdens, and in this way obey the law of Christ. If you think you are too important to help someone, you are only fooling yourself.

GALATIANS 6:2-3

All of you should be of one mind. Sympathize with each other. Love each other as brothers and sisters. Be tenderhearted, and keep a humble attitude. Don't repay evil for evil. Don't retaliate with insults when people insult you. Instead, pay them back with a blessing. That is what God has called you to do, and he will grant you his blessing. For the Scriptures say,

> "If you want to enjoy life
>   and see many happy days,
> keep your tongue from speaking evil
>   and your lips from telling lies.
> Turn away from evil and do good.
>   Search for peace, and work to maintain it.
> The eyes of the LORD watch over those who do right,
>   and his ears are open to their prayers.
> But the LORD turns his face
>   against those who do evil."

I PETER 3:8-12

a. Which passage is the most challenging for you to follow? Why?

b. Write a prayer, asking God to help you in this specific area.

RESPOND

Mentoring is one type of "unlikely" friendship that most people could establish. We both benefited from mentoring relationships during our teenage years.

Our view of God is shaped by different sources in our lives. It could be our parents, a pastor, a teacher, or a friend. My (Trey's) view of God was shaped by a man who never drank alcohol, but who paid for others to go through rehab. My view of God was shaped by a man whose own kids seemed close to perfect, yet he understood and even encouraged the imperfections in other people's kids.

Dick Littlejohn helped me to understand there are at least two ways to view everything—and oftentimes many more. He was never condescending. He was always positive.

He was always comfortable with who he was, and he didn't mind if anyone thought he was eccentric or weird. He had a certain irreverence about him that actually enhanced my faith. In fact, he was the most irreverently reverent man I've ever known.

Because of Mr. Littlejohn, I see people as people, not in shades of skin color. Because of him, I know everyone has the same hopes, dreams, and aspirations, but not always the same opportunities. Because of him, I try to treat the poorest of the poor with dignity. I learned from Mr. Littlejohn that if you're going to help people, help them quietly so they can retain their dignity. Because of Mr. Littlejohn, I felt compassion for both the mother of the victim and the mother of the defendant after I finished a murder trial.

"Anyone can show compassion for the innocent," he would say. "Jesus was compassionate even to those who did wrong."[17]

I (Tim) missed growing up with my father around. So for me, John Moniz came along at just the right time. After flunking out of my freshman year of high school, I was trying to get my life back on track, but I was looking for something I didn't know how to find. Fortunately, my mother continued to believe in me and hold me accountable, and my grandmother was a true prayer warrior. For years, she had been praying my head above water. John Moniz was an answer to her prayers, and he began to work on my heart. He had no ulterior motive. I just knew that he believed in my potential.

I needed good teachers who could help me learn how to listen more than I talk. I needed someone to model leadership for me, to show me how it could be done. John Moniz showed me a world of possibility, and anyone who knew me could see how the trajectory of my life began to change. I learned that it is in my best interest to help someone else before I look for someone to help me. I learned that even a poor kid with no financial resources could make a substantial difference in the lives around him. I learned how to win favor with others by being happy and offering encouragement. I became the most dependable kid in my senior class—the guy who listened to people's problems, who analyzed their options with them and helped them to find a solution. Sometime during my junior or senior year, I began to believe that all things were truly possible.[18]

1. If you have been part of a mentoring relationship, describe the benefits you have experienced or seen. If you have not been part of a mentoring relationship, what benefits do you think such a friendship could bring?

2. Trey's mentor was a man from his church. Tim's mentor was a local businessman who saw Tim at his part-time job. What natural opportunities do you have in your areas of expertise or your local community to mentor a younger person?

3. Are you willing to initiate a mentoring relationship? If so, with whom? What's the first step? If not, why not? What obstacles do you see?

RECONCILIATION IN ACTION

1. Write a commitment statement, sharing your desire to reach across lines of division to pursue unlikely friendships. Outline a plan for how you will begin. Include what you plan to do, how often, with whom, etc.

2. Choose a current friend to act as a sounding board, and agree to check in once a month with a progress report. Commit to sharing what you have done to take steps toward creating your desired vision.

Notes

1. KJV
2. Adapted from Tim Scott and Trey Gowdy, *Unified: How Our Unlikely Friendship Gives Us Hope for a Divided Country* (Carol Stream, IL: Tyndale House, 2018), 27.
3. Adapted from *Unified*, 52.
4. Adapted from *Unified*, 53.
5. Adapted from *Unified*, 11, 87–88, 90–91.
6. Adapted from *Unified*, 19.
7. Adapted from *Unified*, 26–27.
8. Adapted from *Unified*, 93, 165–166, 168–169.
9. Adapted from *Unified*, 97.
10. Adapted from *Unified*, 93–94.
11. Adapted from *Unified*, 105–106, 112.
12. Adapted from *Unified*, 175–177.
13. Adapted from *Unified*, 113–114, 119.
14. Adapted from *Unified*, 133–135.
15. Adapted from *Unified*, 175.
16. Adapted from *Unified*, 179, 185, 193–194.
17. Adapted from *Unified*, 152–154.
18. Adapted from *Unified*, 158–160.

About the Authors

TIM SCOTT is a successful small businessman and US senator from South Carolina. Having grown up in a poor single-parent household, he has made it his mission to positively affect the lives of a billion people through a message of hope and opportunity. He is the first African American to be elected to both the US House and US Senate since Reconstruction, and he currently serves on the Senate Committee on Finance; the Committee on Banking, Housing, and Urban Affairs; and the Committee on Health, Education, Labor, and Pensions.

TREY GOWDY is a former state and federal prosecutor who experienced the criminal justice system firsthand for nearly two decades. In 2010, he was elected to Congress and is now in his fourth term. He is the chair of the House Committee on Oversight and Government Reform and previously chaired the Select Committee on Benghazi. He serves on the House Permanent Select Committee on Intelligence as well as the Judiciary and Ethics committees. He has been widely recognized by law enforcement and victims of crime for his diligent service as a prosecutor.

KATARA WASHINGTON PATTON has written and edited Christian books for children, teens, and adults and created supplemental materials for books by Beth Moore and Joyce Meyer. She served as general editor and writer of *Aspire: The New Women of Color Study Bible*. She holds a master of divinity from Garrett-Evangelical Theological Seminary, a master of journalism from the Medill School of Journalism at Northwestern University, and a bachelor of arts from Dillard University.

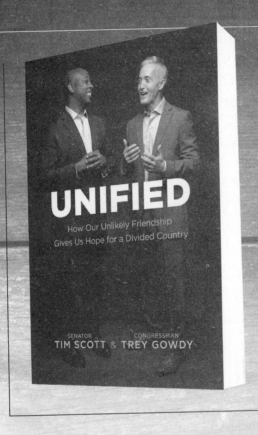